FAMOUS FOLKS
OF AMERICA

LEVEL  READER

3 READING LEVEL · GRADES 2 TO 4

Written by Bethany Snyder and Kathryn Knight
Illustrated by Laurance Cleyet-Merle

Copyright © 2014 Bendon Publishing International, Inc.
All rights reserved. Printed in Haining, Zhejiang, China.

The BENDON name and logo are trademarks of Bendon Publishing International, Inc.
Ashland, OH 44805 • 1-888-5-BENDON
bendonpub.com

GEORGE WASHINGTON

George Washington is called "The Father of Our Country." Do you know why? He was the very first President of the United States.

During the American Revolution against England, he led the Continental Army. After the war, he wanted to help lead his new country and make it good place to live. When other leaders wanted to make George a "king," he said "No!" Instead, in 1788 he was elected as the first President. He won every vote!

George's honesty and courage made him a true American hero. He is pictured on the quarter and the dollar bill. The Washington Memorial is in Washington, D.C.

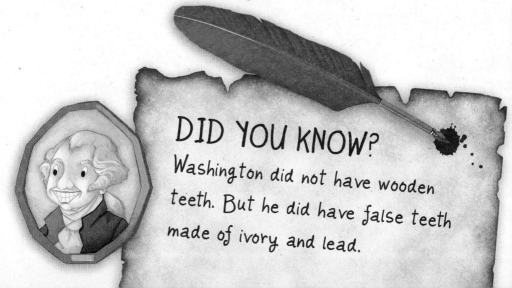

DID YOU KNOW?

Washington did not have wooden teeth. But he did have false teeth made of ivory and lead.

THOMAS JEFFERSON

Thomas Jefferson was born in Virginia in 1743. He was a gifted writer and thinker who wrote the Declaration of Independence in 1776 for the thirteen colonies. He became the third President of the United States.

Jefferson loved to invent, read, and write. He sent about 20,000 letters in his lifetime. When our country's Library of Congress was burned in 1814, it was rebuilt again with 6,700 of Jefferson's own books. Jefferson also started the University of Virginia.

Thomas Jefferson died on July 4, 1826, fifty years after the first Independence Day!

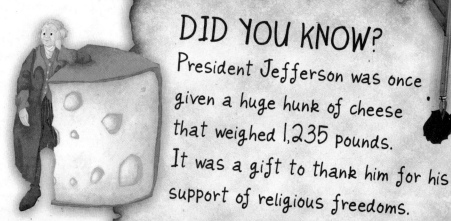

DID YOU KNOW?

President Jefferson was once given a huge hunk of cheese that weighed 1,235 pounds. It was a gift to thank him for his support of religious freedoms.

PAUL REVERE

The British are coming! The British are coming! That was the message of Paul Revere as he raced from Boston to Lexington, Massachusetts, on April 18, 1775.

The 13 American colonies had declared a revolt against British rule. They were prepared to fight for their freedom. Because of Paul Revere's warning, the colonists were ready for the first battle of the American Revolution. The first shot fired, called "the shot heard 'round the world," inspired other nations to seek freedom.

In 1783, the war ended. The colonies won under the leadership of General George Washington. A new country would be born— the United States of America!

DID YOU KNOW?

In 1776, David Bushnell built the first-ever one-man submarine. It was used in New York harbor to deliver a powder-keg "torpedo" to a British ship.

BETSY ROSS

The American colonists wanted to have their own flag. As the story goes, General George Washington knew an excellent seamstress in Philadelphia, Pennsylvania. Her name was Betsy Ross. In May of 1776, Washington took her a flag design and Betsy agreed to sew it.

The flag design had 13 stripes and 13 stars to represent the 13 American colonies. Betsy offered one change. Instead of the stars having six points, she suggested five points. Washington agreed.

On June 14, 1777, the "Stars and Stripes" flag was approved and became our first national flag.

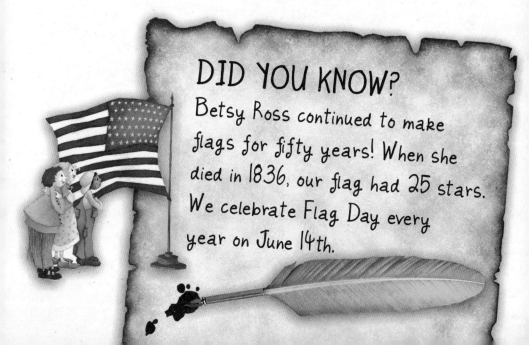

DID YOU KNOW?

Betsy Ross continued to make flags for fifty years! When she died in 1836, our flag had 25 stars. We celebrate Flag Day every year on June 14th.

HARRIET TUBMAN

Our Declaration of Independence proclaims "all men are created equal." However, in the states that allowed slavery, this was not true. There were men, women, and children who were "owned" and could not live as they chose. Many escaped, traveling along secret pathways and following the North Star. These routes came to be known as the "Underground Railroad."

One very brave woman risked her life again and again to help others escape. Harriet Tubman, a slave in Maryland, escaped to Pennsylvania in 1849. She made at least 13 trips back to instruct or lead many slaves to freedom in Canada.

DID YOU KNOW?

Harriet Tubman was the first woman to lead a raid during the Civil War. She guided troops in the Combahee River Raid in South Carolina, rescuing 700 slaves.

ABRAHAM LINCOLN

Do you love to read? So did one of our greatest Presidents, Abraham Lincoln. When Lincoln was a boy he would walk miles to borrow books to read. He had to help his father run their small farm, so he only had time to read late at night by the light of a candle.

President Lincoln led our country through one of its most difficult times—the War Between the States (the American Civil War). He declared an end to slavery. To honor Lincoln, his face is on the penny and the five-dollar bill. The Lincoln Memorial is in Washington, D.C.

DID YOU KNOW?

Lincoln was the tallest U.S. President. He was 6 feet 4 inches tall. He liked to wear his trademark stovepipe hat to appear even taller!

OUR EXPLORERS

As our country grew, curious explorers went out to discover what was in this wide, wild land. They found great forests and huge waterfalls. They found giant trees, hot springs, high mountains, and deep canyons.

Two of our most famous explorers were Meriwether Lewis and William Clark. President Thomas Jefferson sent them out to explore the new Northwestern territories. In 1804, Lewis and Clark set out with a team of men. They followed the rivers and wrote about what they saw—the different kinds of plants, animals, and natural wonders. Lewis and Clark went all the way to the Pacific Ocean and back.

DID YOU KNOW?

American explorers turned their eyes to the skies and wondered: What's up there? In 1961, America sent an astronaut into space. In 1969, American explorers walked on the moon!

OUR PIONEERS

There have been many famous Americans. But this country has also been shaped by regular folks doing amazing things. The pioneers were adventurous people who traveled thousands of miles to settle in new lands of the western territories. They risked their lives, braving vast plains and mountains in heat and snow.

Many pioneers traveled by wagon on the 2,000 mile Oregon Trail that led from Independence, Missouri, all the way to the Pacific Ocean. In 1843, a thousand people made the trip in a wagon train. Over the next 25 years, a half-million people traveled west on the Oregon Trail. They built towns and helped to expand our country.

DID YOU KNOW?

The Oregon Trail was full of pickle-eatin' pioneers. With so few fresh fruits and vegetables, pickles were their main source of vitamin C!

OUR ARTISTS

America has been home to many artists who paint, sculpt, sing, act, dance, design, write, and compose music. Artists have shaped our history and culture.

One famous artist was a poet named Francis Scott Key. One night in 1814, he was being held on a British ship. He watched as the British fired on Fort McHenry, near Baltimore, Maryland. When the firing stopped, Key waited in the darkness.

At dawn's early light, he was full of joy to see the American flag still waving over the fort. Right then he wrote a poem about it. That poem was later put to music and became our national anthem: "The Star-Spangled Banner."

DID YOU KNOW?

Francis Scott Key started writing the poem on the back of an envelope. It was the only paper he had in his pocket!

OUR INVENTORS

Thomas Edison. Ben Franklin. Jonas Salk. Josephine Cochrane. These are just some of the American inventors and scientists that have changed our country—and our world!

Two inventive American brothers gave our country wings. Orville and Wilbur Wright ran a bicycle shop, but they also tinkered with flying machines. Together they built the very first motor-powered airplane. They needed a windy place to test the plane. They chose the sandy dunes near Kitty Hawk, North Carolina.

On December 17, 1903, Orville made the first ever motor-powered flight. It covered 120 feet and lasted only 12 seconds—but that was plenty of time to make history!

DID YOU KNOW?

The young Wright brothers first became interested in flying machines when their father gave them a helicopter-like toy as a gift.

OUR DREAMERS

"I have a dream!" said one man to thousands and thousands of people in 1963. That dream was that one day all people—no matter their color or religion or background—could live in peace. That man was Dr. Martin Luther King, Jr.

Sometimes the greatest ideas begin as dreams. America has always been a land where people could dream big, create, invent, teach, and inspire.

Dr. King taught that we must only fight hatred with love, and never use violence. He was the youngest person to receive the Nobel Peace Prize. We celebrate his life and work every January 20.

DID YOU KNOW?

Young Martin was a very good student. He skipped two grades and went to college at age 15.

When you turn eighteen, you are able
to vote! This means that you—and all other
voting Americans—help shape this great land.
(Maybe someday you'll be famous, and we'll
be voting for you as President!)